Air-Sea Rescue

Contents

Written by Chris Oxlade

Collins

Danger at sea

The first air-sea rescue was in 1911, in the USA. A pilot landed his plane on Lake Michigan, and rescued another pilot who had crashed. Since then, every year air-sea rescue teams rescue hundreds of people who have been in danger at sea. But what kind of dangers do people face?

*Strong winds and enormous waves damage or **capsize** boats, making them sink.*

People have accidents or become ill.

Aircraft land or crash in the sea.

Boats **collide** with one another, hit underwater rocks or have **mechanical** problems.

3

Rescue vehicles and crew

Air-sea rescue crews use different kinds of aircraft and boats to help people who get into trouble at sea. All these craft carry first-aid equipment such as stretchers, blankets and **oxygen** masks. They have **navigation** equipment to find their way, **radar** equipment to spot boats and ships far away and night-vision goggles to help see at night.

Helicopters

The helicopter is the most useful aircraft for air-sea rescue. It can **hover** in the air above a person in the sea or above a boat. Alongside the helicopter pilot, the helicopter will carry a winchman, a winch operator and sometimes a rescue swimmer.

WHO'S WHO

Rescue swimmer

Some air-sea rescue helicopters use rescue swimmers. Helicopter pilots try to get as close to the water as they can, then a rescue swimmer jumps into the water with a life raft, to rescue **casualties**. Being a rescue swimmer is a very difficult job. Rescue swimmers might have to stay in rough sea for up to half an hour.

WHO'S WHO

Helicopter pilot

Pilots need lots of training, skill and practice to keep a helicopter hovering still over the sea, especially in strong winds.

WHO'S WHO

Winchman

A winchman is lowered down from a helicopter on a wire to pluck people from the water, or from the decks of boats. Sometimes more than one person can be rescued at a time.

5

Long-range aircraft

Air-sea rescue crews have long-range spotter aircraft as well as helicopters. Spotter planes fly faster and further than helicopters, and can go hundreds of kilometres out to sea in very bad weather to search for ships and boats in trouble. However, long-range aircraft can't hover in one place like helicopters, so they can't lower a winchman.

WHO'S WHO

Long-range aircraft pilot

Pilots of long-range rescue aircraft have to fly for hours on end during searches and rescues. They have to fly in bad weather and at night. They are normally **military** pilots who do extra training for this special job.

spotter plane

7

Rescue boats

The crews of lifeboats, coastguard boats and other ships often help out with air-sea rescues. These strong boats are designed to go to sea in almost any weather, and they can be **launched** quickly. Like air-sea rescue aircraft, they communicate with other rescuers by radio, help survivors on board and give them first aid. Even submarines have taken part in air-sea rescues!

WHO'S WHO

Rescue boat crew

The crew of a rescue boat are expert sailors. They know how to launch and steer a boat, and navigate to where help is needed, often in very bad weather. Some of the crew members are **mechanics**, who may help to fix boats that have lost power out at sea. All the crew have first-aid training.

offshore lifeboat

Oil and gas disasters

Many people work at sea – in the fishing industry, or transporting goods and people from one country to another by boat or ship. Others *live* at sea, on drilling rigs, which pump up oil from under the seabed. The oil is put in tankers, and then delivered to different countries all round the world.

an oil rig

Oil-drilling rig explosion

The *Deepwater Horizon* oil rig in the Gulf of Mexico was one of the most powerful in the world. Its job was to drill for oil up to 9 kilometres under the seabed. It once drilled the deepest oil well in the world.

When a gas leak caused a huge explosion and fierce fire, many people's lives were in danger. Some of the men jumped into the sea, but others were still on the oil rig.

⚠ DISASTER FACTS

DATE	20 April 2010
LOCATION	Gulf of Mexico, USA
DISASTER	gas explosion, fire
IN DANGER	126 workers

USA

oil-drilling rig →

Gulf of Mexico

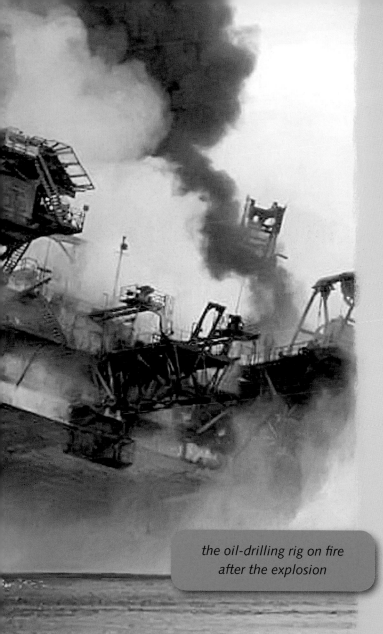

the oil-drilling rig on fire after the explosion

Workers who had jumped into the sea were picked up by an **oil-rig support ship**. From there, crew who were not seriously injured were taken back to shore by coastguard boats. When air-sea rescue helicopters arrived with medical staff, they landed on the deck of the support ship. They then flew 17 injured crew members from the support ship to hospital. But the job of the air-sea rescue crews was not over.

Rescue boats with water-cannon put out the fire burning on the oil rig. Air-sea rescue helicopters searched for missing crew members. When it got dark, special night-vision equipment was used to search a huge area of sea. The rescue crews worked for four days and nights. But sometimes, even with the best equipment, it is not possible to rescue everybody. Eleven people died in the disaster.

Ditching

Aircraft sometimes get into trouble when flying over the sea. If there is a problem with a plane's engine and it can't make it back to land, the pilot may have to make an emergency landing in the sea.

Without a working engine, a pilot must steer the plane at the right angle to land on the water. This is called ditching. If the pilot gets this right, the plane will land safely and smoothly. If the pilot gets it wrong, the plane will crash.

Survivors wait to be rescued from a plane that ditched on the Hudson River, USA in 2009.

A ditched helicopter

In May 2012, a helicopter was heading for an oil rig in the North Sea, with two crew and 12 passengers on board. When the helicopter was 40 kilometres out to sea, there was a mechanical problem with the engines. The pilot deliberately ditched the helicopter into the sea before the problem got worse, which could have led to a crash. Everyone on board climbed into the helicopter's life raft.

> ⚠️ **DISASTER FACTS**
> DATE   10 May 2012
> LOCATION   North Sea
> DISASTER   mechanical failure
> IN DANGER   2 crew and 12 passengers

North Sea

UK

Emergency floats kept the helicopter afloat while the crew and passengers got off.

As soon as the crew sent a **Mayday call**, air-sea rescue helicopters flew to the scene. Two lifeboats were also launched. The first lifeboat arrived within an hour, and the crew helped aboard the survivors who were not injured. When the helicopters arrived, they winched aboard the survivors who needed to go to hospital. Helicopters can travel faster than boats, and they were able to take the injured people to hospital quickly. The successful rescue operation took two hours.

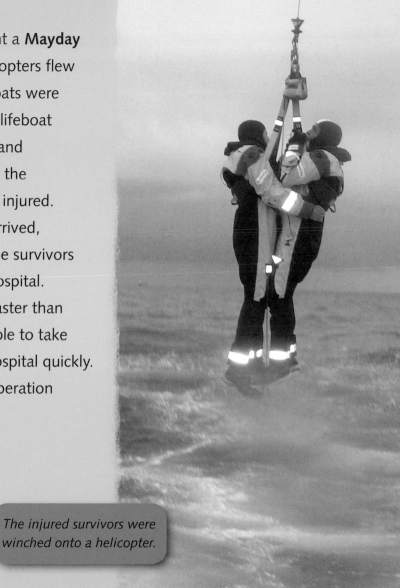

The injured survivors were winched onto a helicopter.

Hitting rocks

Boats and ships working at sea normally follow a set course, using modern navigation equipment. But sometimes, because of engine failure, bad weather or human mistakes, boats and ships hit the shore, or each other.

In 2011, this Chinese fishing boat was stranded on rocks by a severe wind storm.

浙嶺漁

Capsizing boat

A huge hole was made in the hull of a giant cruise ship, the *Costa Concordia*, when it collided with rocks near a small island off Italy. Many of the passengers and crew escaped in lifeboats. Other passengers, who had jumped into the water, were rescued by boat. But some people were stuck on board.

DISASTER FACTS

DATE   13 January 2012
LOCATION   western coast of Italy
DISASTER   collision with rocks
IN DANGER 4,229 passengers and crew

Costa Concordia *disaster*

Italy

Five air-sea helicopters arrived to help. They took it in turns to hover over the ship. Winchmen were lowered down to help survivors, one at a time. Their job was made difficult because it was night time, and the ship was leaning over to one side. A helicopter lifted the last survivor from the ship 36 hours after it tipped over.

air-sea rescue crew rescuing survivors

21

Air-sea rescue – on land!

Air-sea rescue teams don't always work at sea. Sometimes they are needed when people are trapped by floods on land. Their helicopters have the right equipment and trained crew for this kind of rescue.

A man is rescued from a flood in Istanbul, Turkey.

Hurricane Katrina caused floods across parts of Mississippi, USA in 2005.

New Orleans floods

Sometimes, disasters on land affect thousands of people, and many air-sea rescue teams are needed. In August 2005, Hurricane Katrina hit the US coast close to New Orleans. The hurricane's winds caused the sea level to rise so high that water poured over the city's **flood barriers**.

More than 350 rescue helicopters, along with coastguard boats, saved more than 33,000 people in six days. The helicopters winched people from the roofs of houses and buildings, and from road bridges. Coastguard boats can carry more people than helicopters, so they were used to rescue those trapped in their homes.

 DISASTER FACTS

DATE	29 August 2005
LOCATION	New Orleans, USA
DISASTER	flooding caused by a hurricane
IN DANGER	100,000 residents

USA

New Orleans

children being rescued from flooded areas

Unusual rescues

Cable-car rescue

Seventy-five people were rescued from a **cable car**, which had broken down half-way up a mountain.

Animal rescue

A bullock was rescued after it fell over some cliffs.

Ice-box rescue

Two fishermen, whose boat had sunk 25 days before, were rescued from an **ice box**.

In their helicopters, planes and boats, air-sea rescue teams use their skills to find people and take them to safety. Thousands of people have air-sea rescue teams to thank for being alive today.

27

Glossary

cable car   a small cabin hanging from a cable, used to move people up and down a mountain

capsize   turn upside down

casualties   people who are injured in an accident

collide   crash into something (for example, a ship colliding with another ship)

flood barriers   walls that stop a river or the sea from flooding land

hover   stay in the air without moving up, down or sideways

hurricane   a storm with violent wind

ice box   a big box for ice, to keep fish that has been caught fresh

launched   got out on to the sea

Mayday call   a call for help from a boat or plane

mechanical   to do with machines

mechanics   people who maintain or mend machinery

military   from the armed forces

navigation   finding the way from place to place

oil-rig support ship   a ship that takes supplies and equipment to oil rigs

oxygen   a gas that we need to breathe

radar   a machine that shows where ships and aircraft are, even at night

Index

Saving lives at sea – and on land

Rescue vehicle	Rescue crew
Helicopter 	<ul><li>pilot</li><li>winchman</li><li>rescue swimmer</li></ul> 
Lifeboat 	<ul><li>boat crew</li><li>mechanic</li></ul> 
Long-range spotter aircraft 	<ul><li>pilot</li><li>pararescue crew</li></ul> 

Disasters

- **aircraft ditching**
- **boats hitting rocks**
- **flooding**
- **oil rig explosion**
- **animal rescue**
- **cable-car rescue**

- **aircraft ditching**
- **boats hitting rocks**
- **flooding**
- **oil rig explosion**

- **ice-box rescue**

Ideas for reading

Written by Clare Dowdall, PhD
Lecturer and Primary Literacy Consultant

Learning objectives: identify and make notes of the main sections of text; use syntax, context and word structure to build a store of vocabulary; use the language of possibility to investigate and reflect on feelings, behaviour or relationships

Curriculum links: Citizenship; Geography

Interest words: capsize, casualties, coastguard, collide, flood-barrier, hover, hurricane, launched, Mayday, mechanical, mechanic, military, navigation, radar

Resources: whiteboard, ICT

Getting started

- Ask children to look at the front cover together. Discuss the title, *Air-Sea Rescue* and challenge children to describe what they can see happening in the picture.

- Read through the contents together. Ask children to suggest what each section might be about and what rescues it might contain, e.g. rescuing people from flooded houses, and make notes on the whiteboard.

Reading and responding

- Turn to pp2–3. Ask children to identify new and unfamiliar words, e.g. mechanical, collide. Remind them of the range of strategies for decoding and understanding new vocabulary, e.g. phonic strategies, associating parts of new words with words that are familiar.

- Using pp2–3, model how to read the information provided and identify the main aim of the pages, e.g. that this section will describe the reasons people need to be rescued by crews. Explain to children that by doing this you are summarising the most important information.

- Ask children to continue reading to p27 in pairs, supporting them to make meaning as they read by asking questions and discussing the events being described.

Returning to the book

- Return to the notes made on the whiteboard. Explore whether children's ideas about each chapter reflected the content of these sections and discuss their new knowledge of each topic.